Focus on

The Poetry of Tony Harrison

Sean Sheehan

GREENWICH EXCHANGE
LONDON

Greenwich Exchange, London

Focus on
The Poetry of Tony Harrison
© Sean Sheehan 2008

First published in Great Britain in 2008
All rights reserved

Printed and bound by Q3 Digital/Litho, Loughborough
Tel: 01509 213456
Typesetting and layout by Albion Associates, London
Tel: 020 8852 4646
Cover design by December Publications, Belfast
Tel: 028 90286559

Greenwich Exchange Website: www.greenex.co.uk

Cataloguing in Publication Data is available from the British Library

ISBN-13: 978-1-906075-15-6
ISBN-10: 1-906075-15-8

Contents

1 Speaking Your Mind   1

2 Kumquat Days   31

3 Harrison Remains Too   40

Glossary   44

Further Reading   47

Index of Poems   48

1

Speaking Your Mind

Central to Tony Harrison's poetry is the importance of being able to speak your mind and express your sense of being. He is very much a public poet, someone who wants to speak on matters both intimate and political that concern us all. His poetry also explores the reservations and doubts that lie behind the seemingly laudable notion of saying what you mean, hesitations that ultimately point to a void in our sense of being. 'Saying what you mean', calling a spade a spade, may seem perfectly to line up intention, meaning, and performance – the voice as a vector of the mind that always points forward with clarity – but the process of articulation is not such a straightforward matter. It is usually a social and interpersonal event and there is, after all, the addressee to take into account and the effect of what is said on others.

Speaking your mind can be a blunt business and may not always be the most considerate way to express yourself: someone may be hurt by not having their feelings taken into account. In relation to one's own self it may, paradoxically, be a misleading guide in terms of being true to yourself. To speak your mind may speak a brusqueness or infelicity that ideally you did not intend and the result may be something more, or less, than what you desired. Speaking too explicitly may result in a surplus of meaning that fails to capture what you are trying to express; speaking too indirectly can create a looseness that slackens the focus and sidelines meaning. Sometimes the most appropriate form of expression is silence, the kind that is said to speak louder than words, and it may be your silence, or the silence of others, that you seek to give expression to. To be articulate about the inarticulate, whether the unspoken belongs to someone else or to a decentred part of yourself, involves problematic issues of subjectivity and identity that are explored by Harrison.

Subjectivity, the sense of me the subject as an 'I', seems to be the integrated motor that drives the speaking of one's mind and the expression of an identity. But is the core of the subject, that which remains when all the speaking is bracketed off, anything more than an empty space that cannot articulate itself? In his *Memoirs of Dadaism*, Tristan Tzara recalls his reading aloud of a newspaper article at an event, while an electric bell kept ringing so that no one could hear what was being said. The audience – becoming exasperated and annoyed, calling for an end to the performance – did not understand "that [all] I wanted to convey was simply that my presence on the stage, the sight of my face and my movements, ought to satisfy people's curiosity".[1] The audience sought a deeper satisfaction, the confirmation of a full subject capable of richly expressing itself. Such a richness being seen and heard in the act of expression would bear witness to the presence of an active agent, one capable of bearing a meaning that could go to the heart of subjectivity and affirm its totality. Such a sought-for satisfaction may be doomed to failure. The subject is always displaced in the act of representing itself in language, endlessly seeking a signifier that is authentically 'his own' but necessarily excluded from articulating such a fullness of being because it is not there in the first place. The result is always a failure, either by saying too much or too little, and the kernel inside the husk of the subject is just this lack. What defines the subject is the hopelessness of the endeavour and Harrison's poetry can be read as an enactment of this endeavour and its hopelessness.

Speaking your mind is not the same as your mind speaking. The notion of the mind speaking can suggest a disembodied voice, the mouthpiece for something that is really mental and profoundly interior, and this may encourage or endorse the idea of the mind's separate identity from the body. The mind may then be viewed as something non-material and non-physical, and this way of seeing the relationship between mind and body, what in philosophy is called Cartesian dualism, strikes the wrong note if used to approach Harrison's poetry. The importance of avoiding such a dualism is that in a non-Cartesian world, where body and mind are parts of a physical and social whole, speaking your mind is inseparable from speaking your voice. Voice is the machinery of the tongue moving within the mouth and at the same time it is the body's expression of itself as an individual and as a social being. A term from literary criticism, 'discourse', is appropriate here because its view of language as both material and social, and not as something abstract or disembodied, brings the reader closer to an understanding of Harrison's work.

For Harrison, born and brought up in a working-class district of Leeds, a northern vernacular was and remained his natural way of speaking even though his education widened his understanding of discourse. As a schoolboy in a grammar school in the 1950s, the subject matter of the first part of 'Them & [uz]', his Yorkshire pronunciation of a Keats poem, earned rebuke from an English teacher who labelled him a 'barbarian' – the ancient Greek term for anyone who was not a Greek, the word capturing what to them was the meaningless noise ('bar-bar') of any language spoken by a foreigner – and the teacher castigated Harrison for mangling the true voice of English:

> Poetry's the speech of kings. You're one of those
> Shakespeare gives the comic bits to: prose!

Literary art is deemed to be beyond him, literally unspeakable. It is seen to belong more naturally to the class of those who rule and wield power, the 'kings' of a Shakespeare play. The pupil in this classroom does not heed the admonition and goes on instead to learn something the teacher never intended: that poetry need not belong to only a few, and literary art can be a weapon with which to fight back and usurp the usurpers.

Challenging concepts of the ownership of language becomes a political act because ownership itself is being challenged. Like squatters making better use of a building than those who merely hold a lease on an empty property, the territory of poetry can be disputed:

> So right, yer buggers, then! We'll occupy
> Your lousy leasehold Poetry

and the second part of 'Them & [uz]' proclaims the speaker's intention to speak as a poet in his own voice, for himself and his class. How, though, given the sophisticated codes, the traditions and conventions of this language form we call poetry, will he be able to give voice to those who are excluded by these codes? How can the silence of those who do not have a voice in poetry be broken without assimilating them into a class that prides itself on keeping them out as a mark of its own difference?

The ramifications of Harrison's intention and the difficulties this engenders are far-reaching, and the result is poetry that flows along branches that lead into colonial, national, local and family history as well as politics, language, and culture. The complex ways in which these branches interweave with one another are rooted in his own experiences. He was born in 1937, two years before the start of the Second World War, and early memories include the celebratory bonfires that were lit to celebrate the end of the war in 1945. As a teenager, and very much against the odds for someone from a working-class home, he won a place at Leeds Grammar School and went on to study Classics at university.

Three hundred years before Harrison's time, there was a young man in southern England who also had a knowledge and love of Greek and Roman literature and who also decided, probably against the wishes of his father, to become a poet. This was John Milton, who went on to write 'Paradise Lost' and ardently speak out for the republican cause in the English Civil War of the 17th century, though his radical politics tend to be downplayed when his status as one of the greatest English poets is conventionally evoked. In one of his early Latin poems, 'Ad Patrem' ('To My Father'), Milton addresses his father and offers his poem as a thanksgiving and expression of the filial obligation he feels. The poet has nothing else he can give, any wealth he may possess lies with his poetry, and Milton ends by hoping his praise and memory of his father will serve in a future age as an example of personal fidelity. Harrison uses the opening and concluding lines of this Latin poem as a dedicatory piece to his own *School of Eloquence* poems and they appear after a quotation from E.P. Thompson's *The Making of the English Working Class*. Thompson's ground-breaking work of history traces the early development of a working-class consciousness, beginning his account with the formation of the working men's London Corresponding Society in a London pub in 1792. By situating his own poems in a sense of history, Harrison is evoking another Milton, the one who in his Latin poem attributes his poetic inspiration to Clio, the Muse of History. Both poets see their work as interwoven with a sense of history.

Harrison has no problem assimilating the private Milton, the poet-son of 'Ad Patrem', with the politically engaged public writer. Quite the opposite, for part of Harrison's admiration for Milton is his ability to deepen the relationship between poetry and history:

> I think how Milton's sonnets range from the directly outward to the tenderly inward, and how the public address of the one makes a clearing for the shared privacy of the other.[2]

This remark of Harrison's highlights the way his own poetry blurs any simple boundary between the political and the personal. It is something that is readily apparent in the first poem, 'On Not Being Milton', in *The School of Eloquence*, a sequence of sonnets mostly written between 1986 and 1990. Harrison calls this first poem his *Cahier d'un retour au pays natal* (notebook of a return to a native land), the title of a prose piece by Aimé Césaire about the liberation of the black population of Martinique, and he dedicates his poem to two members of Frelimo, the Mozambique liberation movement. At the same time, the poem is a very personal declaration and serves as an introduction to what he is going about in the poetry that follows.

From Africa 'On Not Being Milton' moves to northern England and the Luddites' battering of the machinery that is depriving them of a livelihood. This is a political act and its significance merges with their demotic language: the stress of their blows with the Enochs a counterpart to the stresses of the "glottals" and "morphemes" of their spoken tongue. In this way, language and action perform together an enunciation, an 'articulation', of their class identity. This is succinctly conveyed in the wordplay on the "looms", referring to both the machines the Luddites smash and the 'owned language' they challenge by their own way of speaking. Using a metaphor in this way continues the trope of the previous line where "the frames of Art" also conjure up more than one referent. The frames point to parts of the machinery but also to the way in which some forms of art are expropriated and thus awarded the capitalised status of Art by those with cultural power. Such forms are maintained exclusively by a minority as a mark of their difference and assumed superiority – a frame both contains and excludes – and Milton, the radical republican who has become a conventional figure of Art, has been unjustly assimilated in this way.

In this sense Milton has been 'framed' and set up as a paradigm of high Art. This could provide a way of reading a sub-text into the poem's title, the negative state of *not* being Milton a way of asserting Harrison's intention to dissociate his work from that exclusive realm of art into which Milton has been unfairly incorporated. At the same time, though, Milton's presence in the poem is a positive act of inclusion and his voice is more an echo of solidarity than opposition.

The negative in the poem's title may be read as an expression of modesty, the writer acknowledging the 17th-century poet's unique achievements and not claiming to be another Milton. He is also saying, given the historical changes since the 17th century, that he cannot be another Milton. He is not getting too big for his boots but, instead, setting out to find a means of expression that fits him, one that can relate to black history as much as to his own country's history. In his local Leeds area, England's history includes the Yorkshire miners blackened by the coal dust of their working environment; so when he speaks of "growing black enough to fit my boots" the national and international are both present as echoes of the poet's intention to be inclusive.

The poem also contains an allusion to an English poem, Gray's famous 'Elegy Written in a Country Churchyard', about the way the fact of death equalises all lives. There are people buried in the churchyard who did not achieve or seek fame in their lifetimes – "Some mute inglorious Milton here may rest", records Gray – and Harrison echoes this in his "Three cheers for mute ingloriousness!" but not in the quietist tone of the 18th-century poet. This aspect of Harrison's use of Gray will be looked at in more detail later.

A feature of *The School of Eloquence* poems, beginning with the E.P. Thompson and Milton quotations and confirmed in 'On Not Being Milton', is what literary criticism likes to call heteroglossia, a hybrid of different voices or languages within a text so that no single utterance assumes dominance. The Soviet philologist who coined this term, Mikhail Bakhtin, also introduced the concept of dialogism. This is the idea that no word or verbal declaration can stand alone, because they are subject to a process of refraction through other voices. The result is that every text is multilayered with echoes of other, sometimes contrary, texts. This facilitates an approach to literature that allows for a variety of different readings. In what used to be called post-structuralist or deconstructionist criticism, it allows for an open-ended, asocial exploration of the fluid, unhinged foundations of language. A system of linguistic signs becomes a discourse, defined by its textuality and dialogic relations, free from any notion of an unmediated, stand-alone truth.

The danger with this kind of literary criticism is that the more it explores the instability of language the more it can divorce itself from the solid ground of material reality and social history. When Luddite or African history, Latin, French, Greek, and Roman or Yorkshire colloquialisms feed into Harrison's verse he is not celebrating the flux of language for its own sake. '*Fling our doors wide! all, all, not one, but all!*', the triumphant call at the end of 'Wordlists III', may sound as if this is what he is doing but only when the line is taken out of the context and its political implications not taken on board. Harrison does not celebrate language for its purely intrinsic worth, words are more than words – "society's not like the *OED*" – because they are bound up with history and class, and in welcoming linguistic diversity he is simultaneously expressing a political point of view.

In 'The Rhubarbarians', the barbarians of the classroom from 'Them & [uz]' are cloth workers, croppers, gathering in a field at night in preparation for an attack on Rawfolds mill in 1812.[3] History records actual words spoken by mill owners like Horsfall of Ottiwells, who had a cannon mounted in his mill to protect it from attack, but not those of the Luddite croppers whose political discourse, conducted in their vernacular, was far from being the incomprehensible crowd noise of the kind that actors make on the stage by repeating "rhubarb". The speech of the Luddites, sounding "rebarbative" to some, articulated their discontent and their resolve to try and save their means of livelihood. Unlike what schools inculcate, they were not parroting conformist talk about '*rege et lege*' (king and law) when, enacting their opposition, they set off for the mill armed and noisy with "the *tusky-tusky*" of their pikes.

In an interview,[4] Harrison connects the poem with his father's memory of being in a school production of *Julius Caesar*, his lowly role being to hold a spear and mutter "rhubarb, rhubarb, rhubarb". The poet knows there was far more to his father than this, but, like the Luddites, his parent belonged to a class of people denied expression by their place in a particular cultural and political order. The result can be a form of self-censorship, a state of mind that discourages speaking out, and a retreat to a self-effacing silence. In a society deeply and damagingly divided by class, those who lack social power are relegated to a cultural underground and their voices are not easily heard. The poet does not know what the croppers, brushed aside and quietened ("parries and hush"), said to "soldier, scab and sentinel", but their dialect is a reminder, a 'remembrancer', of who they were, how they spoke and what they stood for. It requires an effort to recover their presence and their articulacy for, like the figures in the poem playing the traditional game of knurr by the light of the moon, only shadows indicate their existence. The need for this effort to be made is enacted in reading the poem for there is an initial difficulty discerning what 'The Rhubarbarians' is about. In the first quatrain, especially, the syntax seems ungainly – as does the non-standard English of the Yorkshire vernacular – and until you get your head and your tongue around it, there is a difficulty in understanding the poem.

Speaking his mind in solidarity with those who are effaced, in 'Remains' Harrison tells the story of how literary tourists visiting Wordsworth's cottage in the Lake District do not see there the single line of poetry penned by the decorator who hung the wallpaper. The cultural tourists cannot see this act of trespass "nailed behind a shutter" as they "traipse" around on a literary pilgrimage, but the poet identifies himself as the 'restorer' who will find his own voice through the marginalised W. Martin:

> I use
> the paperhanger's one known extant line
> as the culture that I need to start off mine.

Visitors to the cottage seek a ready-to-imbibe improvement of their minds and a refinement of taste and manners, but the poet, using at first the term "culture" in the biologist's sense of a medium for cultivation, finds there instead a way of nurturing an alternative culture.

This alternative to what is deemed artistically edifying will not readily be accepted by the upholders of Establishment culture but the poet accepts this: "then hide our combined labours underground." He knows too that the cultural order can erase completely the voice and language of the powerless, and the poem that evokes this with the example of the Cornish language, 'National Trust', concludes with the knowledge that control over language is a way of ruling and exploiting others. This is also the concern of 'On Not Being Milton' where the reference to "branks" – a device fitting around the head and having a metal bit which fits over the tongue to prevent speech – is a metaphor for this.

Issues of language and silence run through the *School of Eloquence* sonnets, accompanied by a range of emotions from tenderness and pity through to self-disgust, anger, and grief. An example of how such conflicting feelings can be expressed and controlled is 'Marked with D.', a poem about the poet's thoughts at his father's cremation. It is an elegy, a song of lamentation and a very personal one, shot through with a grim humour that helps control the unhappiness. The sardonic tone is registered in the opening two lines, noting how the "chilled dough" of the corpse resembles the material that his father worked with daily as a baker. The religious imagery that follows could sustain a belief in the next world but the metaphors are not allowed to do this, the flames are only to be taken "literally", and the bathos that comes with the line ending on the word "sorry" is redeemed by its repetition at the start of the next one and the qualification that this entails. Sonnets in the Italian form are usually divided into two parts: an octave (eight lines) which presents the subject matter and the conflict or problem it gives rise to, and a sestet (six lines) which then resolves or comments upon what has gone before. 'Marked with D.' modifies this traditional form by using sixteen lines, Harrison's characteristic form for sonnets, but the last four lines follow the convention by offering some kind of resolution. The wordplay returns to the world of the bakery but this time to deliver an angry rebuke: it was the culture and social codes of his country that made his father feel unworthy, and the personal shifts to a more public statement.

Harrison's liking for the sixteen-line sonnet comes from the extra flexibility it allows for, and part of the pleasure in reading these poems comes from appreciating the deftness and power with which he handles the form. A good example of this is the use of single lines in 'Study' and the summation that comes in the singular, final line:

My mind moves upon silence and *Aeneid* VI

This line and the poem as a whole is about the unspoken but, while this is overtly signified by the uncrying of the dead new-born baby, the reluctant inarticulateness of Uncle Joe, and the muted clock, there is a deeper silence that comes from contemplating the mystery of life and death. In the sixth book of Virgil's *Aeneid* the hero visits the underworld and witnesses a world of non-existence, and the poet ends 'Study' by thinking of this in the silence of the empty room. Some things are best expressed by saying nothing, just like the great moments that Yeats refers to in his 'Long-legged fly' as being inextricably bound up with the absence of speech – "Like a long-legged fly upon the steam/His mind moves upon silence" – and Harrison explicitly evokes this insight and mystery in the last line of his poem. There is a deeper silence, too, in the poem: the impossibility of finding a signifier that would be the subject's own because of the lack, the void of meaning, that constitutes the subject in the first place:

The settee's shapeless underneath its shroud.

Silence is central to Harrison's poetry, and this conjunction of the unspoken with the spoken is not the paradox it seems. Nor should this vital aspect of his work reduce the *School of Eloquence* poems to the level of sociological material about estrangement through education in working-class homes. If the poems could only make sense and possess a value on this level their worth would be much diminished, but this is not the case because the poems, while obviously shaped by the particular circumstances of Harrison's own life, are about what language cannot include, and this cuts across social class while at the same time being conditioned and shaped by class.

What is this limit of language, that which it cannot include? As an end point that cannot be crossed by language, it naturally resists any easy articulation. Like the hole in the doughnut, it is an emptiness that constitutes the identity of that which surrounds it, a space that helps define presence.[5] In 'Wordlists II', Harrison ruefully notes the different languages he can handle while acknowledging what remains beyond his grasp:

> but not the tongue that once I used to know
> but can't bone up on now, and that's mi mam's.

This is not tear-jerking sentiment about an educated adult forlornly aware that his working-class roots have been severed, although it can be read as such, but an acknowledgement of the loss, or fissuring, of identity and the awareness that somewhere outside of the poet there is an elusive truth about himself. The articulation of this something that is missed in his own subjectivity is what he seeks, and the absence that he experiences cannot easily be expressed in language. Paradoxically, the perfect iambic pentameters of the two lines above can only calmly highlight the inexpressibility of what he is seeking.

Similarly in 'Book Ends', there is the straightforward, sociological reading of the poem that readily lends itself to a sentimental interpretation of the poet's unhappy plight. Yes, father and son are divided by education and cannot easily communicate despite their common grief, but this is not necessarily the heart of the poem. It may lie somewhere else, to be sought in the insistent rhythm and stark stresses of the verse:

<pre>
    /   /   /   /   /
Baked the day she suddenly dropped dead
    /   /   /   /   /
we chew it slowly that last apple pie.
</pre>

The syntax of the opening is deliberately disconcerting so as to displace attention onto what was an act of the living but is now permanently in the past. It is over and done with, as utterly finished as the being of the person who made the pie, and the shocking finality of death is enunciated in the emphatic stress of the opening syllable and the funeral pace of the stresses that follow. The silence of death unites them as much as "books, books, books" divide them, and in their own different ways they both confront the limits of language.

Left like this, though, the poem can still be reduced to just a liberal humanist reading, and the deeper cause that lies behind the disturbance of the father–son relationship remains a too-familiar and superficial one about death and mourning. Evoking an educational divide and repeatedly summoning books as an explanation for their plight is a displacement effect for a cause that cannot directly be addressed. This cause, touched on by the trauma of the death in the family, is the awful emptiness that gapes in the middle of the symbolic order. There is a void, a lack in the subject's sense of self, that resists the symbolic order of language; it is the lack around which language is incapable of symbolising, and the son is using books as a substitute object to plug the gap in his own and his father's sense of being. What they seek is some sense of self-identity, something that the dead woman provided by framing them as book ends and seeing them as identical despite differences, and her death has exposed the void.

Some of the concerns that have so far been touched on come together in 'v.' in vigorous and exciting ways, and the poem's achievement and limitation can be approached by looking at the form of the poem. It is composed along the lines of Gray's 'Elegy Written in a Country Churchyard', four-line stanzas of iambic pentameters with an *abab*

rhyming scheme, a poem that Harrison evoked in his earlier
'On Not Being Milton'. The poem 'v.' is also an elegy of sorts,
a lamentation for the state of Britain as well as his parents'
grave, and the setting is similar even though it shifts from
a rural to an urban cemetery. The similarities are fascin-
ating because of the way each poem, in its own way, works
within and against its form. In his *Some Versions of
Pastoral*, the literary critic William Empson famously
analysed how a verse in Gray's poem betrayed an ambiguity
that undermined its stated purpose:

> Full many a gem of purest ray serene
> The dark, unfathomed caves of ocean bear;
> Full many a flower is born to blush unseen
> And waste its sweetness on the desert air.

The lines are illustrating Gray's general point that the self-
effacing people buried in the graveyard of a small village
may not have attained worldly fame or riches but this fact
does not detract from the quality they brought to their
existence. The lines in question, by way of analogy with a
valuable gem in an unknown cave and a lovely flower that
blossoms unseen, are saying how lives of anonymous
individuals, like those whose graves he contemplates, could
have risen to greatness were they not constrained by their
humble environment. However, as Empson shows, the
graceful nature of the verse exalts their unfortunate
circumstances and inclines the reader to accept their plight
as something desirable and unchangeable. The imagery
draws on facts of nature which suggest this is the way things
should be: a gem does not seek removal from its cave and a
flower is happy to remain unseen and unplucked. The word
"blush", suggests Empson, hints at virginity and a laudable
state of renunciation. In this way, the language works
against the argument; the rural poor are not really
disadvantaged and there is no reason to feel aggrieved at
waste of talent and lack of opportunity. The elegant flow of
iambic pentameters carries a gentle rhythm that supports
the status quo and invites the reader to engage and indulge

in a wistful melancholy. The way in which the poem speaks subverts the surface meaning; form and content are at odds with one another.

A verse from 'v.', though written in the same form as Gray's poem, achieves a radically different meaning because of the way (as well as in its very obvious use of a dissimilar diction) it works metre and mood, rhyme and rhythm. Iambic pentameters provide the underlying metre of the poem and the *abab* rhyme scheme is a constant but the rhythm – the varying flow of the lines and the changing pattern of stressed and unstressed syllables – follows with energy the speaking voice of the colloquial. Harrison handles this tension between metre and rhythm, between rhyme and diction, with a skill and imaginative force that is exciting, creating the provocative tone and texture that are so characteristic of the poem as a whole. The following lines from early in the poem serve as an example:

> This graveyard stands above a worked-out pit.
> Subsidence makes the obelisks all list.
> One leaning left's marked FUCK, one right's marked
>   SHIT
> sprayed by some peeved supporter who was pissed.

The secure and comfortable metre of this verse sets the graveyard scene, but there is nothing cosy or bucolic about it: headstones in danger of collapsing veer away from one another as if themselves inebriated, and iambs starkly register the swear words they now bear. This is not Gray's quiet churchyard but a Britain deeply divided by class, in the midst of the miners' strike of 1984–5, where the National Front can recruit from the ranks of the unemployed and the embittered. The skinhead whose words appear in italics speaks for disaffected youth and for the working-class class anger of 'rhubarbarians' but he also speaks for the self-interrogating poet. These voices battle and collide with the metre of traditional English verse, rudely challenging but not destroying it:

/ / / / / /
So what's a cri-de-coeur, *cunt? Can't you speak*
/ / / / / /
the language that yer mam spoke. Think of 'er!
/ / / / / /
Can yer only get your tongue round fucking Greek?
/ / / / /
Go and fuck yerself with cri-de-coeur!

The French term, literally 'a cry of the heart', is ironically apt as a way of describing the skinhead's genuine declaration of class-warriorship. A scan of these lines reveal how this defiance expresses itself in the rhythm. The first line begins smoothly with three regular iambs before being suddenly broken with the emphatic stress on the demotic, disrupting the measure of the metre but rhythmically hugging the contours of the colloquial. What is also disrupted is the aesthetic of the shocked liberal voice that had earlier, and so earnestly, questioned the cause of the vandalism. The question posed by the skinhead touches a nerve in the poet, for the mention of his mother's language echoes the lament of 'Wordlists II', and it is the angry youth who is championing his mother's dialect by his use of "yer" and "'er".

Oppositions are exposed throughout 'v.' with a verbal and metrical brilliance that makes the poem a pleasure to read aloud:

Vs sprayed on the run at such a lick,
the sprayer master of his flourished tool,
get short-armed on the left like that red tick
they never marked his work much with at school.

The verve of the iambic pentameters re-enacts the racy style of the graffiti sprayer, and the rhyming of monosyllabic beats – "at such a lick/like that red tick" – drives home the irony behind the fact that finally, and despite his poor schooling, the skinhead has achieved some eloquence and artistry of self-expression.

How, though, are we to read the conclusion that the

battered poet reaches after he leaves the cemetery and returns home? The intellectual and emotional bruising that he has received from the subversive articulacy of the skinhead has until now been the central current of the poem, and it can also be understood as a conversation taking place in the poet's head as he reflects on the divisive nature of his society, the role of poetry and, more personally, his relationship with his neighbourhood and his parents. In the poem, he returns home and finds solace in the warmth of a coal-fuelled fire, listens to music with his partner and watches the news on television. In 'Book Ends' the gas fire in the room could not serve as a means of comfort, but in 'v.' a fire is part of the warm environment that serves as refuge from the enmities broadcast on the television. The miners' strike is mentioned, among other conflicts, but these are not dwelt on and he turns away from them to a private and amorous peace:

> Turning to love, and sleep's oblivion, I know
> what the UNITED that the skin sprayed *has* to mean.

The placing of "*has*" in italics and the stress it receives in the line emphasises the word's importance and draws attention to the uncertainty and the fragility behind the urgent need for the comfort that the poet goes on to attach to his private relationship. There is a degree of desperation in his attachment to the solace offered by his home life, marked in the poem by the "Home, home to my woman" refrain that is repeated once too often for real assurance. Instead of – but not a million miles away from – the quietist resignation of Gray's poem, 'v.' concludes with a world-weary withdrawal from political divisions, an escape into the soothing comfort of his partner and a humanist elegy that is unconvincing:

> but leave, with the worn UNITED, one small v.

> victory? For vast, slow, coal-creating forces
> that hew the body's seams to get the soul.

The question mark in the second line is much needed, for what exactly is Harrison turning to here? Geomorphology was an earlier link between the romantic warmth of the home fire, the coal mine beneath the cemetery he has vowed never to return to, and the news about the miners' strike that was on the television. Now, there is some vaguely metaphysical elegy to the nature of time and the way in which its slow process, by affecting everyone, becomes a unifying force. If this is what is meant then it is not too dissimilar to the philosophical mood of Gray's poem. It is a turning away from the political and from the class war of the miners' strike – and this is disappointing – even though, or because, the poet is aware of another voice that insists on making itself heard:

> The ones we choose to love become our anchor
> when the hawser of the blood-tie's hacked, or frays.
> But a voice that scorns chorales is yelling: Wanker!
> It's the aerosolling skin I met today's.

The intimate fraternity of personal relationships will not ultimately suffice to unite the oppositions that the poet has confronted, and at the very end of the poem it is the messy materiality of "beef, the beer, the bread" that situates him and provides his epitaph and not, thankfully, some sentimental and Hardyesque trope about time. The poem's political intelligence resurfaces at its conclusion, and the optimistic possibilities that might lie behind the letter of the poem's title, when 'v' stands for victory, are treated with a necessary circumspection.

'Initial Illumination' also considers the nature of victory, this time the one claimed by the US in the first Gulf War, and does so by a series of images that skilfully interweave and turn back on themselves, illuminating the hypocrisy behind the religious rhetoric of George Bush senior and his government. The use of imagery displays a verbal intricacy that mirrors the visual elaborations found in the manuscripts of monks – the subject matter occasioned by the poem's opening picture:

> Farne cormorants with catches in their beaks
> Shower fishscale confetti on the shining sea.

There is a clarity to the language here that matches the sharp focus of the scene. The haiku-like description of the cormorants wastes no words: the first line is a statement of fact, followed by a simple but startling image that brings the moment to life. A spirit of celebration is evoked by the confetti image, and it might at first seem to suit the poet's mood as he takes in the bright view from his train. He is heading north through Northumbria and past Lindisfarne, the island where monks once lived and laboured in a time labelled the Dark Ages. While there is actually very little to celebrate there is much to reflect on, and images of light and dark work off each other throughout the poem: the darkness of contemporary history as the US destroys Iraq, raining down bombs that radiate in the night sky and deceive cocks into crowing; the visual illumination that monks brought to words of the Bible as opposed to the obscuring cover that religion provides for those who kill in the name of God; the headlights of vehicles versus the blackened bodies of burnt victims and, returning to the poem's opening, healthy cormorants that could shower shimmering fishscale now dying in the oil-polluted, "black lacquered sea". The self-glorifying acclamations of the victors, not just the US but all those who celebrate in triumph over their wars won, are seen as a dark achievement of the night. Like the 'short-armed' version that the skinhead sprays in the Leeds churchyard, the V for victory proclaimed by the US is also lacking something ("Is it open-armed at all") despite the "trumpets bulled and bellicose and blowing" – the alliteration here helping to enact the bullying, bull-like ("bulled") assertion of raw power.

The title of 'Initial Illumination' at first refers to the beautifully decorated letters of monks' manuscripts, but it also describes the opening bursts of bombing that light up Baghdad's night sky. Given the reality of the war and the reasons for it, the title also serves as an ironic epitaph for the proffered but ultimately false light of reasoning employed by warmongers. In this way, the title captures in essence the verbal dexterity and discipline that make this poem so effective. Occasionally, the language of a Harrison poem risks becoming too convoluted or too intellectual for its own good, but 'Initial Illumination' maintains its focus through its brilliantly handled imagery.

There is, though, in 'Initial Illumination', the possibility of a lapse in the language and because it may also be a weakness in tone it is not easy to separate the form from the content. The lines in question come towards the end of the poem:

> let them remember, all those who celebrate,
> that their good news is someone else's bad
> or the light will never dawn on poor Mankind.

The thought being expressed seems a bland and ineffective one, as if a gentle reminder to the Pentagon to show a little enlightenment will help in the progress of humanity. The limp humanism of these particular lines is in danger of weakening the poem's incisive critical edge. What could be savage irony behind the mention of "their good news" – this being the etymology of 'gospel' – is displaced by the rest of the line. Similarly, although the light/dark contrast in the following line ties in with the rest of the poem, it comes out sounding pitiful rather than political. Fortunately, this is not the tone of the poem as a whole and 'Initial Illumination' concludes with the image of a crowing cock standing on a dunghill as an emblem of the acclaimed US victory.

'A Cold Coming', paired with 'Initial Illumination' in Harrison's *Collected Poems*, also deals with the first Gulf War in 1991. Expressed in equally strong verse, though this time in a series of rhymed couplets, the poem is a response to a powerful photograph that was published in *The Observer* showing the charred upper body of an Iraqi soldier leaning against the windscreen of the truck in which he has been incinerated.[6] The animating force that drives the power of the poem calls to mind what Freud says in 'Timely Reflections on War and Death', written in the middle of the

First World War. He predicts that if the slaughter on the battlefields of war should ever conclude the victorious combatant will "return cheerfully home to his wife and children, unchecked and undisturbed by thoughts of the enemies whom he has killed", and he contrasts this likelihood with primitive cultures where the returning victor cannot enter his village until he has expiated the murders he has committed. At one level this is just a superstitious fear that the spirit of the slain may seek revenge, but "the spirits of the slain foe are nothing but the expression of his bad conscience over his blood guilt; behind this superstition there lurks a piece of ethical sensitivity which civilized people like ourselves have lost."[7]

Harrison thinks it is time for the ghosts to return, and the "scorched vocal chords" of the dead Iraqi speak into the poet's recording device. The soldier has heard of the "three wise Marines' banking their sperm before leaving for battle – a way of preserving their lives before setting out to destroy others" – but, in line with the superior technical capability that gives military victory to the US, the means of doing this are not available to him:

> Sad to say that such high tech's
> uncommon here. We're stuck with sex.

Harrison wants to restore for the "devotees of 'kicking ass'", British *Sun* readers as well as the American public, the ethical dimension which Freud says modern warfare is able to erase. Were the poem to receive a public broadcast, it is appropriate to imagine Harrison reading his lines against a backdrop of a magnified image of the *Observer* photograph (a photo that was self-censored by the American press).

As with 'Initial Illumination', though, a liberal platitude risks weakening the power of the poem with Harrison's insistence that the reader take note of Iraq's attack on Kuwait and the Scud missiles "launched against the Jews" by Saddam. Such references are politically correct at best; at worst they blur the issues behind the war. The invasion of Kuwait was the 'cause' of the war in the sense that the assassination of an Austrian archduke was the 'cause of the First World War. "Jews" nicely completes the couplet by echoing "excuse", but lines with a rhyme for Israel would have been more insightful. As it stands, the couplet risks confusing the causes of European anti-Semitism with those pertaining to the Middle East and the reasons for Arab hostility to Israel. There is a symmetry to the poem's central trope in the "bottled Bethlehem" as an image of a hoped-for world renouncing war – pacifist semen kept in cold storage until the time is right – but this poetic piety is too close to the kind of blather about the need for peace that is rhetorically employed by the very powers who conduct the war. Far more telling is the symmetry that emerges from the last lines of the poem: pressing the rewind button so as to return to the Iraqi ghost.

Twelve years after Operation Desert Storm, the rewind button is pressed by the US and the UK in the second Gulf War, and this time Harrison's political intelligence is not dulled in the slightest. 'The Krieg Anthology' continues a tradition that harks back to Shelley's 'The Mask of Anarchy', written shortly after the Peterloo massacre of civilians in Manchester in 1819. Shelley's fury is directed at those responsible, and he wants to name names:

> I met Murder on the way –
> He had a mask like Castlereagh –
> Very smooth he looked, yet grim;
> Seven blood-hounds followed him:

Castlereagh was Foreign Secretary and the dominant member of the reactionary government that condoned Peterloo, and in 'Baghdad Lullaby', in the same angry spirit and employing the same rhyming scheme, Harrison names Geoffrey Hoon, Defence Secretary in 2003, when the bombs rained down on Iraq:

> Sshhh! Ssshhh! Though now shrapnel makes you shriek
> and deformities in future may brand you as a freak,
> you'll see, one day, disablement's a blessing and a boon
> sent in baby-seeking bomblets by benefactor Hoon.

Sarcasm is stirred with a dour humour when Blair is ventriloquised in 'Holy Tony's Prayer':

> At Camp David dinner I say grace
> with my most holy parson's face.
> Though brother George requires no prod
> To bring your name up often, God,

and this blend of anger and ridicule is a characteristic of Harrison's overtly political poems that works to good effect. In the anti-royalist 'A Celebratory Ode on the Abdication of King Charles III' there is a flight of imagination that allows the poet to bemoan the time it has taken Britain 'to become a republic: Why has it taken all this while/desceptring this sceptred isle'?" He celebrates the long-awaited maturity of the nation and with cheerful, but pointed humour, points out that, should the monarchy ever be restored, Ted Hughes (Poet Laureate at the time) would probably have to deliver an appropriate verse and be suitably rewarded with a lordship. It would be a mistake to take the poem's humour as indicative of a lack of depth on Harrison's part. He may be good-naturedly making a dig at Ted Hughes for accepting the laureateship and at Richard Eyre for accepting a knighthood – awards bearing a royal premise – but he is making a serious point when he looks forward to the dropping of the prefix 'Royal' from institutions like the National Theatre (of which Richard Eyre was a director). The monarchy has no real political power but a strong ideological role that taps into a hidden realm of fantasy by providing people with an appeasing sense of identity, and this makes it difficult to challenge. Fantasy need not always be used as a counterpoint to 'reality' and can be viewed instead as a way of structuring reality through its ability to fix the psyche with particular subject positions. Harrison hints at a psychoanalytic way of understanding how Britain's monarchy survives by referring to the infantile nature of its support – the country forgoing the chance "to be a grown-up girl" and delaying the onset of "an adult state" – and the use of "Sirs and Dames" to provide contentment.

He situates the "taste for fawning" within the minds of those who find something satisfying about the monarchy, inviting an approach that could label the royal acronyms and the 'Sirs and Dames' as simple examples of what Žižek calls *object little a* (see glossary).

Harrison wants to remain a churl – a term from monarchist vocabulary for a man without any rank – but he does not want to fall into the trap of appearing churlish by expressing anger. Instead, he sensibly points out that work is its own reward and no more needs royally appointed titles to recognise its worth than it requires a *king*dom. Remove the monarchy and the United Kingdom (UK) does deserve the prefix 'Former' – so "the acronym comes out as FUK!"

After the death of Hughes, Harrison was the logical successor to the laureateship . When this was raised publicly the very possibility that he might accept royal patronage aroused his ire and found apt expression in his faxing to a newspaper 'Laureate's Block', dedicated to 'Queen Elizabeth', most of which had been written earlier when the death of Hughes brought home to Harrison the need for an end to the post of Poet Laureate. Compared to 'A Celebratory Ode on the Abdication of King Charles III', this poem's more sustained assault on royalty succeeds as a first-rate polemic. The humour is more subversive than before, not least in the way it takes on board the fantasy element that sustains the language of royalty – not, this time, through the bestowed identities of Sir, Lord, Dame, and so on but in the master signifier itself: Queen Elizabeth. Harrison is in Stratford with his partner, an actress playing a part in a Shakespeare history play, and she is the Queen Elizabeth he looks forward to being in bed with, celebrating the company of an equal rather than 'fawning' before a sublime object of ideology.

It is worth returning to 'A Cold Coming' because of the way the poem itself returns the reader to Harrison's 'The Nuptial Torches' from his early collection *The Loiners* that was published in 1970. The most disturbing poem from that collection, 'The Nuptial Torches', is a first-person narrative by Isabella of Spain describing the mass burning of heretics on the day of her marriage to Philip II. It shares with 'A Cold Coming' an insistence on the barbarism, expressed graphically and sensually, of extreme political violence. The burning flesh of Carlos de Sessa "spat like wood" and body parts of Ponce de la Fuente are "hacked off", and such matter-of-fact descriptions are matched in 'A Cold Coming' by the "scorched vocal chords" and the "skull half roast, half bone" of the dead soldier. The two poems also share a macabre conjunction of sexuality with violence in very precise terms. In the earlier poem, burning flesh drops from the body like "bed clothes off a lovers' bed" and 'A Cold Coming' calculates the number of Iraqi war dead by way of a sperm count. More generally, the poems are united by their fixation on fire as a reminder of all that is grossly enacted by two seemingly very different historical events. In 'The Nuptial Torches' fire consumes the victims of the Inquisition but it also fuels the lust of the perverted Philip and his relishing of violence and pain. His sexual sadism is also expressed in images of fire and flame:

> These nuptial nights,
> Crackling like lit tapers in his tights,

Fire consumes the Iraqi soldier in the Gulf War but this poem, focusing on the victim rather than the perpetrator, uses fire imagery to convey the horror of the needless loss of something precious:

> I was filled with such a yearning
> to stay in life as I was burning

and it is given a dramatic and uncomfortable reversal when it is used to drive home an important message:

> Don't look away! I know it's hard
> to keep regarding one so charred,
> so disfigured by unfriendly fire
> and think it once burned with desire.

More comprehensively, fire serves to align the abuse of political power with a willingness to countenance terrifying acts of barbarism. In the age of the Inquisition this willingness was enacted by incorporating the burning of bodies into the spectacle of a royal wedding; centuries later, in the age of another Christian empire, a homology can be traced in the endorsement of a relentless bombing of a country from the air that results once again in charred bodies. The reader of Harrison's poetry, returning to 'The Nuptial Torches' after 'A Cold Coming', moves back through history and makes connections between events across time.

A similar movement occurs when reading the third part of 'The White Queen', another of Harrison's early poems with an historical setting. Syphilis is brought to Europe as a result of imperialist adventures in the New World of the Americas and the disease becomes a metonymy for the consequences of the greedy plundering of the resources available in the new continent. In 'Shrapnel', the last poem in *Collected Poems*, Harrison is prepared to accept the possibility that the area where he lived as a child escaped being bombed through a humane decision by a Luftwaffe pilot to drop his deadly load on a nearby park instead. The houses that survived became homes for new generations of families:

> Our house, thanks to that humane bombardier,
> still stands; and those of Hasib mir Husain,
> Mohammad Sidique Khan, Shehzad Tanweer.

'Shrapnel' concludes with 'Tanweer', one of the three British citizens, listed here, who blew themselves up in London on 7th July 2005, rhyming with 'bombardier' – a disquieting reminder of the 52 people who died in London as the result of bombs that did not miss their targets. Given the likelihood that the bombers' sense of grievance was related to the government's foreign policy and its war in Iraq, the 52 victims are also charred victims of a war in the Gulf. In this way, the poem ends with a chilling echo of the prophecy made in the third part of 'The White Queen' – that imperialism will exact a price and "crimes abroad [will be] brought home as civil war."

Imagery relating to fire is a constant in Harrison's poetry and at its most general serves as an intensifier to the particular subject matter of a poem. It would not be difficult to draw up a long list of his poems that feature fire, sometimes as a central and unifying metaphor as in 'Marked with D.' or 'Fire-Eater'; at other times as a single image within a poem, as in the "shirt of Nessus fire" in 'A Kumquat for John Keats'; and sometimes as a solitary occurrence as in the first line of 'On Not Being Milton'. An explanatory force for this may be located in a remark of Harrison's about how when he looks into his childhood for something that would explain why he turned to poetry " … my images are all to do with the War."[8] He goes on to recall particular childhood experiences of the Second World War:

> One of my very earliest memories is of bombs falling … Another is of a street party with a bonfire and such joy, celebration and general fraternity as I have never seen since. As I grew up the image stayed but I came to realise that the cause of the celebration was Hiroshima. Another is the dazed feeling of being led by the hand from a cinema into the sunlit City Square after seeing films of Belsen in 1945, when I was eight.[9]

The bonfire street party was a VJ event on 15th August 1945, the day victory over Japan was celebrated in Allied countries (nine days after the first atomic bomb was dropped on Hiroshima). Belsen, although it was never a Nazi death camp, was a concentration camp liberated by the British in April 1945, and newsreel of what they encountered there – thousands of unburied dead, mass graves, and emaciated victims dying of typhus and starvation – was shown to a shocked British audience. Hiroshima and the Holocaust, twinned by the use of fire on a scale never previously imagined, entered the consciousness of a young boy in Leeds, and they have never ceased haunting it.

In the first part of 'The Morning After', the VJ bonfire

leaves a "dark, scorched circle on the road", just as Hiroshima and the Holocaust burn themselves into the conscience of the poet. The representation of a rising sun on the Japanese flag is erased by the flames of the celebratory bonfire but something horrific, not known to the youngsters at the time, has also been registered:

> The Rising Sun was blackened on those flames.
> The jabbering tongues of fire consumed its rays.
> Hiroshima, Nagasaki were mere names
> for us small boys who gloried in our blaze.

When pronounced as trochees, the words 'Hiroshima' and 'Nagasaki' puncture the regular iambics of the previous lines, suspending the rhythm so as to announce starkly their significance before allowing the verse to resume its customary pace in the line that comes after and return the reader to an innocent scene of children around a bonfire.

The fact that Hiroshima and the Holocaust happened undermines the innocence in Harrison's memories of childhood and challenges any view of the world that evades confronting this fact. Language itself can be at a loss when it comes to comprehending these events, and in 'First Aid in English', a poem that cleverly makes this point, the last verse drives home a further realisation: Hiroshima and the Holocaust are not just events that can be bracketed off from the history we now inhabit. The blanks and ticks of the last verse signify the possibility that there will be more acts of genocide and more uses of atomic weapons:

> Cats in their clowder, lions in their pride,
> but there's no aid in English, first or last,
> for a [Fill in the blank] of genocide
> or more than one [Please Tick] atomic blast.

and Harrison's poetry explores what it means to live with this knowledge. The starting point is the need to acknowledge the openness of history and the realisation that there are no certainties, ideals or objects of fantasy that can fill the void. 'Old Soldiers' uses the label that used to appear on bottles of Camp coffee extract to express the sense of metaphysical loss that this realisation induces. The colourful label featured a Sikh, standing before a seated Scottish officer, bearing a tray with a bottle of the coffee extract.[10] The label on the picture of the bottle depicted the same scene; and so, in theory, the scene was repeated ad infinitum "down to amoeba, atom, neutron size". In a safe and innocent world, of the kind that the poet could imagine he was once part of as a child, the iconic scene did more than evoke the certainty of Empire. It represented – or, looking back on his childhood, it now comes to represent – a secure sense of one's place in the order of being, a stability at the heart of everything. It is this sense of primordial belonging, of knowing how we fit into the ontological whole, that has been shattered by the traumatic significance of Hiroshima and – implied by other poems – the Holocaust.

This could lead to a nihilism, an extreme cynicism, or a confirmed misanthropy but Harrison rejects such positions and, in the culture of ancient Greece, finds sustenance for a life-affirming philosophy that can be sustained in the face of Hiroshima and the Holocaust. By allowing for passion, but without sacrificing the horror, the Greeks also enable him to go beyond the sometimes too schematic nature of poems like 'First Aid in English'.

Notes
[1] Edmund Wilson, *Axel's Castle* (Fontana, 1962), pp.239-40.

[2] www.contemporary writers.com

[3] Croppers were skilled workers who prepared rough cloth by shearing its surface. For an account of their work and Luddite activism, see E.P. Thomson, *The Making of the English Working Class* (Gollancz, 1963), pp.521-52.

[4] Richard Hoggart, 'In Conversation with Tony Harrison', *Bloodaxe Critical Anthologies. 1. Tony Harrison*, ed. Neil Astley (Bloodaxe, 1991), p.39.

[5] The image comes from Sarah Kay, *Žižek* (Polity Press, 2003), p.4.

[6] The photograph can be seen at http://news.bbc.co.uk/2/hi/middle_east/4528745.stm

[7] Sigmund Freud, *On Murder, Mourning and Melancholia* (Penguin, 2005), pp.189-90.

[8] *Bloodaxe Critical Anthologies. 1. Tony Harrison*, p.32.

[9] Ibid.

[10] The label on Camp coffee extract was changed in 2006 to show the Sikh solider sitting down alongside the Scottish officer and sharing their drink. The bottle on a tray bearing the same label no longer appears.

2

Kumquat Days

Harrison was introduced to Greek literature and language at school and he went on to study Classics at Leeds University, the beginning of a lifelong immersion in an ancient culture that has profoundly affected his poetry and his philosophy of life. His knowledge and respect for the ancient Greeks has blended seamlessly with his proletarian politics and in a way that subverts the relationship usually perceived to exist between Classics and class. Knowing the Classics was part of the domain of a mandarin class, and even today familiarity with the subject still tends to be a characteristic of a privileged education, and a certain kind of elitism remains associated with the mindset of the classicist, if only in the popular imagination. Harrison is one of the many who disproves this unhelpful generalisation, not least in the way his poetry mixes the classical and the colloquial in ways never previously imagined. In 1985, amidst the media-driven rumpus over 'v.', when he was President of the Classical Association of Great Britain, Harrison wrote to *The Times* replying to "the letter from Mr Hector Thomson affirming the central role of Latin in the continuity of English literature … I am very glad to be able to endorse all he said by swearing, if I may be permitted, that without the many years I spent acquiring Latin and Greek I should never have been able to compose my poem v." Such wit and wisdom about the meeting of contraries is itself a feature of the Greek world, and Harrison has attested to aspects of this on a number of occasions. In a 2007 interview he spoke of how he liked that image of a theatre in the open air, staged in the full light of day, not in darkness. Actors and audience illuminated by the same light. No lighting system but the sun. Not a solitary people in front of a television screen under some illusion that a whole nation is being addressed. No, the whole of one culture gathered in the morning ...[1]

In the glare of the sun, masked figures explored the dark side of humanity – war, murder, lust, revenge, incest – and performances of tragedy were followed first by satyr plays, where characters familiar from tragedy mixed with choruses of phallus-wielding satyrs, and then full-length comedies.

The ancient Greek view of life appeals to Harrison because of the way it confronts the horrors of existence without flinching or turning aside while at the same time living with the transitory joys that a new day may bring. His remark that "what we can learn from the Greeks, is an ability to think the worst things that can be thought without giving up on life"[2] serves as a way of understanding the philosophy that is given expression in 'A Kumquat for John Keats'. Having reached middle age and knowing "that it's too late for dying young", he is pleased to be alive still but very far from feeling complacent. He lives with uneasy truths that place him on a precipice from which it would be easy to fall over and embrace forgetfulness through death. Events of a personal kind, in his case the death of his mother and the recent near-death of his daughter in a traffic accident, can turn everything so sour that even "the very sunlight made me weep". He thinks of his fellow poet Keats who died at little over half his own age and yet knew about the precariousness of happiness and life's sadness always lurking in the background. Two lines from Keats' 'Ode on Melancholy' – "Aye, in the very temple of Delight/Veil'd Melancholy has her Sovran shrine" – are directly referred to, and Keats comes again to his mind when contemplating the kind of dread that the younger poet was spared from acknowledging. In 'Ode on a Grecian Urn', Keats could explore aspects of life by contemplating the art of an ancient culture, but modern history, imagined as an infernal crater "with bloody bubbles leering at the rim", seems to mock such fond aspirations. Atomic bombs, so relatively small in terms of their destructive power as to be likened to an urn, utterly subvert notions of truth and beauty that existed before the weapons' use in the Second World War. Keats began his poem addressing "Thou still unravish'd bride of quietness,/Thou foster-child of Silence and slow Time", but what happened in Japan in 1945 savagely "ravishes all silence and all odes". The lines that follow conjoin figures of classical mythology with images of Hiroshima and Nagasaki victims: the Roman goddess of flowering, Flora, is choked by contaminated air; the nymphs of rivers and springs, Naiads, thirst for water while Dryads, nymphs of the wood, are limbless in a landscape denuded of trees; children die in an agony of fire like Hercules, who burned himself alive to escape the terrible pain from the shirt that had been soaked in a poison created by Nessus. Hell is on earth and – this is the bedevilling dialectic – so too, on some days, is heaven. The heavenly bliss of being alive and sentient can be as acutely joyful as the awareness of what Harrison calls 'Nothingness', and the poem evokes both through the unifying experience of biting into and eating a kumquat. The fruit and its sweet-and-sour taste captures the strange co-mingling of melancholy and merriment in life:

> /   /   /   /   /
> Then it's the kumquat fruit expresses best
> /   /   /   /   /
> how days have darkness round them like a rind,
> /   /   /   /   /
> life has a skin of death that keeps its zest

The regular iambic pentameters pause at the end of the second line and the key subject, "life", comes to the fore when the reader's attention is caught by its unexpected stress at the beginning of the third line; the other four stresses in this line beat out the singular and stark metaphysical message.

The anti-Cartesian stance of 'A Kumquat for John Keats', its refusal to divide the intellectual from the sensual, is echoed in a remark Harrison made in an interview:

> ... my head faces human history, and has a very bleak and pessimistic view of the possibilities for mankind, while at the same time I am very conscious of having a very sensual, celebratory nature; much of my work seems to be a confrontation of the two.[3]

This helps make sense of two lines in the poem:

> History, a life, the heart, the brain
> flow to the taste buds and flow back again.

expressing how body and soul register and respond to contradictions and contrary impulses: the sublime taste of a strange fruit, the misadventures in spelling by greengrocers, the elation of waking to a fresh morning in Micanopy in Florida and feeling glad to be alive yet fully aware of the horrors of history. He is, after all, living in the one country that has dropped atomic bombs on civilians. The poet's imagination affects his feeling, he cannot separate the sorrow from the joy that are both deep in his flesh and in his mind, and finds it difficult not to wince at the sheer beauty of a Galway landscape when lit by the sun after prolonged rain. The propinquity of pain and pleasure is tasted in a fruit where you cannot "say where the sweetness or the sourness start".

The zest of life is hard to feel in the face of hard facts, whether political ones of a global kind or personal tragedies as with the death of someone close. Confronting such stubborn realities is a state of mind that one lives with. There is no choice, and the only opt-out lies with a willingness to succumb to self-delusion and fall prey to the ready availability of manufactured illusions. There are any number of difficulties to deal with. One is the challenge of facing up to unavoidable aspects of history like nuclear weapons and the Holocaust. Another is the sheer meaninglessness of existence, the loneliness we try to escape from but will finally face when our own death approaches. Then there is the temptation to succumb to illusionary forms of happiness of the kind that religion offers. Harrison finds expression for some of these difficulties in metaphors of weather and climate. Such imagery is appropriate given the way meteorological patterns are often regular and constant but always susceptible to an underlying unpredictability that is capable of disrupting such patterns.

In 'Facing North', the north wind signifies those hard facts that we have to live with and 'weather out'; when the wind blows the paper lantern in his draughty room everything seems unstable:

> Now years of struggle make me concentrate
> when it throws up images of planets hurled,
> still glowing, off their courses, and a state
> where there's no gravity to hold the world.

North is a metonymy for all that threatens hope and contentment and it is only by facing up to ontological anxiety that the poet can calm the mental tumult and "focus on an Earth that still has men,/in this flooded orchestra". The earliest known resolve to confront the anguish of existence was played out in Athenian drama, in a semicircular space called the orchestra, lit ("flooded") with the natural light of day, and 'Facing North' is about carrying on in the existentialist spirit of the ancient Greeks. What also helps is the company of someone to love, in this case the woman on the other side of the Atlantic who has received the poet's many airmail letters. At the end of the poem he leaves the room, presumably in the northern city of Newcastle and presumably setting off for that warmer clime where his loved one is. The wind, though, will continue to swing the light bulb and the North, as the epigraph from the poet Louis MacNeice makes clear, will still be a part of his consciousness.

In 'Florida Frost', the assault on one's ability to cope with the irrational and the inexplicable is told in the personal tragedy of a woman's unexpected death from cancer and the severe shock experienced by her husband who struggles to control his grief. Just as the warm climate of Florida can suffer a spell of freak coldness, happiness can be shattered by the death of someone loved. The harsh cold damages the kumquat – "ice-candied rind/rims the ruined kumquats" – and the precarious balance that the fruit was able to represent in the earlier poem is lost. The kumquat becomes like the pomegranate that was fed to Proserpine (the Roman version of Persephone) by Pluto (a name for Hades, the god of the Underworld). To maintain the poem's rhyme and rhythm, Harrison uses the less familiar names, but the myth being evoked is that of Persephone, unable to return to earth with her mother because the young girl had eaten pomegranate seeds, and that is enough to tie her to the Underworld for a part of every year. Humanity is wedded to death just as "sad Proserpine" is married to Pluto.

Such philosophical ruminations are a feature of the poems Harrison wrote in the United States, and in 'Skywriting' there is a clear indication that the concern with such reflections is being focused by his sojourn in American society. In this poem, abstract philosophising comes down to Californian earth as the poet contemplates the glass-top surface of his desk. Gazing at the desk, he can see reflections of class activities occurring across the street from where he sits and he can also make out on its surface the smoke trails of a skywriting plane. He is reminded of Pasedena's New Year Rose Parade, and in a virtuoso linguistic display – the language is flowery in more than one sense of the word – the floats of the street parade are described in all their showy excess:

> A woodwardia howdah delicately sways
> with jonquil rajahs turbaned with bouquets,
> the Cross in crocus and in baby's breath
> but no carnation Christ clamped to his death,
> no battered nailheads of black onion seeds,
> no spearthrust of poinsettia that bleeds.

The show exults in a visual sumptuousness: giant woodwardia ferns form a howdah – a canopied seat of the kind that adorns ceremonial elephant parades in India – and yellow jonquil flowers shape human figures that become rajahs, bearing turbans of more flowers in bunches. One of the floats bears a representation of the Christian cross, formed from crocuses and the small white flowers called baby's breath, but this is a sanitised image for there is no figure of the crucified, bleeding Christ. This critical observation – why represent the cross and not the body crucified on it? – is driven home by noting what could have been added but instead has been left out: no clusters of black seeds that could have served for the nailheads, no use of the poinsettia's bright red leaves to indicate the wound caused by the soldier's spear. This is a Disneyland cruci-fixion, and the self-indulgence that is conveyed in the over-the-top flowery language is subverted by the rhymes that change from a graceful "sways/bouquets" to the unsettling "breath/death" and "seeds/bleeds". There is a falsity to the parade because its celebration of life is superficial, an act of denial about the darker aspects of existence that is matched by the celebrants choosing to ignore the fate of the flowers the day after the parade. The ebullience of the skywriting turns to cloud, day turns to night, and the shiny desk top now reflects the darkness as the poet peers into its shiny blackness. Like Narcissus staring at his own image in water and oblivious to all else, the sombre poet ignores the celebrations on the street outside; his spirit is drawn to the "dark depths" of the glass desk and he "stares at seas of ink".

In Greek myth, the flower that grew up on the spot where the handsome young Narcissus fell in love with his own image was named after him. At a naturalistic level, as the name of one more type of flower, the narcissus has an acceptable place within the poem's floral pantheon. The figure of Narcissus, though, becomes a richly suggestive one in 'Skywriting'. The poet is compulsively drawn to the darker side of life and will continue to be so until, as the poem's last line suggests, he dies. In this way he resembles the young man of Greek mythology who pined away in the one spot by the water's edge. The merrymakers, too, bear their own resemblance to Narcissus for, just as the young man fell in love with the loveliness of his own face, the American public indulge in self-congratulatory celebrations that ignore certain realities and at a cost to their own ultimate worth. Narcissus-like, their egotism is doomed to wilt, and the conquering spirit that sends rockets into "half unconquerable space" calls for a critical intervention. Like the Arabella spider sent into space by NASA to see if webs could be spun in a weightless environment, the poet seeks to weave connections between aspects of the culture he inhabits and his own sense of human limitation and death.

In 'The Call of Nature', the poem's droll couplets and its witty title satirise what was the underlying source of the poet's discontent in 'Skywriting' – a lack of authenticity in the way some people live their lives – and connect the dearth of experience with a consumerist mentality. Yet the two poems are very different. In the earlier one, the density of the language, the tightly packed images, and the complexity of the narrator's angst work together to create a tone of intellectual gravitas. 'The Call of Nature' is sharper in its focus and the poem's pace is quicker – the narrator's consciousness is not an issue here; hence the absence of metaphysical worries. The difference between the two poems is reflected in the sparse landscape of 'The Call of Nature' that contrasts so dramatically with the elaborate, florid pageant of the earlier poem:

> Juniper, aspen, blue spruce, just thawing snow
> On the Sangre de Cristo mountains of New Mexico.

The matter-of-fact tone suits the pragmatic concerns of the literary tourists and the reified nature of their world. Similarly, the verse proceeds at a jaunty, no-nonsense tempo and the easy-to-read lines reflect the vacuity of the tourists' mind:

They've heard about his work, and that it's rude.
Back on the valley freeway at the first motel
they forget both noble Navajo and D.H.L.

– and the poem's final couplet expresses with sarcasm the
hollowness of their experience.

Notes
[1] *The Independent*, 7th April 2007.
[2] Richard Hoggart, 'In Conversation with Tony Harrison', p.42.
[3] John Haffenden, 'Interview with Tony Harrison', *Bloodaxe Critical Anthologies. 1. Tony Harrison*, p.227.

3

Harrison Remains Too

In a 2007 newspaper article entitled 'Only Pinter Remains', Terry Eagleton noted the seemingly terminal decline of the long tradition in British literature of a radical questioning of the foundations of the western way of life.[1] From the early days of Britain's emergence as a capitalist industrial state, beginning with Blake and Shelley, there were literary voices opposing the dominant order, and the dissent of writers can be clearly traced through the 20th century. The occasion for Eagleton's gloom was the recent knighting of Salman Rushdie, someone whose writings once satirised the West but now, having embraced the reactionary politics of American neoconservatism, are a source of dismay. Eagleton detects a similar trajectory of decline shaping the work of the playwright David Hare and the novelist Martin Amis. Only Harold Pinter is singled out as an honourable exception amongst contemporary writers. This is premature: Tony Harrison's voice should also have been accorded a place and his direct lineage with Shelley celebrated.

Harrison's poetry, like Shelley's, is didactic and political in the fullest and most positive senses that can be brought to these terms. Both words come from ancient Greek: didactic from the verb for 'to teach' and politics from the Greek word for citizen and the city-state. Harrison wants to understand the nature of the society of which he is a citizen and his understanding, which is also a learning process, is something he shares with the readers of his poems. All poetry has an effect on us, this is the poet's intention, and what matters in a qualitative sense is the nature of this effect and how it is produced. In the ancient world that gave us the terms *didactic* and *politics*, the study of how language produces its effects was called rhetoric, and to read Harrison as a rhetorical poet is to enjoy the art he brings to speaking his mind. He speaks with eloquence, he does not preach or bully, nor does he relinquish the command of rhythm that lies at the heart of poetry. The result is superb verse that combines intellectual muscle with the blood of emotional engagement, a body of verse that thinks and feels with gusto.

It is because he is speaking his mind about how we live, as social beings with finite lives, that his verse never becomes so quiveringly introspective and private as to disengage itself from encountering the real. In equipoise to this political and public side – and forming with it the essence of Harrison the poet – is an abiding concern with the solitary self trying to come to terms with the nature of existence. This is the poet of 'Skywriting' who sees himself like that first spider sent into outer space, grappling with the nature of physics and selfhood:

> the creator with small letter c,
> to learn to spin new webs in zero G.

The rhymes of this couplet evoke the realm of physics (the speed of light and zero gravity), but the intention being expressed is a metaphysical one. An engineer of poetry, he seeks to employ the creative faculty in order to confront life, and enlightenment comes not from the carousing crowds on the streets but from accepting the dimension of radical negativity and creating meaning where, ultimately, no meaning exists:

> The tarred creator stares at seas of ink,
> and at the solstice of his silence cries aloud:
>
> The Pasedena HAPPY turns to cloud!

The writing in the sky was a visible attempt to suture the negativity and, just as visibly, it fails before his eyes.

The conclusion of 'Skywriting' is the realisation that he will go on repeating the same cry "until the seas of ink have all run dry" and the same compulsion is to be found in 'Two Poems for My Son in his Sickness'. In these poems, the father–son positioning that was a feature common to much of his earlier work undergoes a grim reversal as the poet as father lays bare his anguish at the plight of his son's mental illness. In the first of the two poems, 'Rice-Paper Man', he confesses how in the desperation of grief he found himself resorting to futile measures: lighting a candle in a Spanish church, throwing a coin into a wishing well in Romania, scapegoating a rice-paper man at a Japanese temple. Berating himself for falling prey to superstition, he turns instead to language to assuage his pain. He confirms in verse his resolve, however awful the predicament, never to turn to the falsity of religion as a prop. He cannot help but trust in the possibility that by speaking his mind and expressing his misery there is some shred of comfort to be gleaned. The second poem, 'Sugaring the Pill', dilutes even this hope. When his son was a child the father could sugar medicine for him by mixing it with jam, but now their roles reversed, the son has grown up and has to take "the bitterest pill" whole while the father is "too full of gall to swallow even mashed in verse". Yet the writing of verse must go on. Language, his poetry, becomes a simple persistence against the odds and in continuing to craft his poems he echoes the perseverance that Samuel Beckett also enshrined in his art: "in the silence you don't know, you must go on, I can't go on, I'll go on."[2] Let us, though, give the last word to the last words of 'Rice-Paper Man':

> The question is: Do you think poetry,
> specifically *this* poem, was worth a try?
> If not, and you found no comfort, not one phrase
> to brave *memento mori* and *olés*,
> or redeem doomed spermatozoa, drive
> a stake through this undead art and you'll survive.

Notes

[1] *The Guardian*, 7th July 2007, p.36.

[2] Samuel Beckett, *Trilogy* (London, Calder Publications, 2003), p.418.

Glossary

alliteration: the recurrence of the same or similar consonant.

bathos: a descending movement from the elevated and sublime to the commonplace or ridiculous.

bucolic: relating to country life, the pastoral.

demotic: belonging to ordinary, common people, often referring to their speech.

dialogism: the dynamic total of language possibilities inherent in any cultural discourse.

didactic: concerned with the teaching of a lesson.

discourse: language as a signifying system between human subjects situated within a particular field (e.g. the literary, the medical, the political) which is determined by historical and social factors.

elegy: a lament for the dead, from an ancient Greek word for a poem of mourning.

heteroglossia: an effect of dialogism, the way language is stratified by any number of different dialects, jargon, and other forms of speech.

homology: a relation of sameness by way of a structural correspondence.

iambic: referring to a foot (metrical unit) of two syllables, with the stress occurring on the second syllable, e.g. 'to be' and 'or not' in the first line of Hamlet's soliloquy: "to be or not to be, that is the question".

iambic pentameter: a metre of poetry made up of five iambs, though not necessarily pronounced in this way. "To err is human, to forgive divine", for example, has ten syllables made up of five iambs but one would not normally pronounce the line strictly in accordance with its metrical pattern.

metonymy: the representation of something by another thing which is associated with it or is a part of it, e.g. 'crown' for 'monarchy'.

object little a: a term used by the philosopher Slavoj Žižek in his account of the way an object can be invested with a psychological significance that comes from its ability to embody a lack in our ecology of being; an *object little a* being a substitute object that plugs the gap in our sense of being that seeks an undivided self-identity.

ontological: the adjective of 'ontology', the study of the nature of being (alive).

post-structuralism: an approach to literary criticism, also called deconstruction, based on the importance given to the signifier (word or sign pattern) as independent of the signified (concept). The arbitrary nature of language is stressed so that the play of language becomes divorced from the external world and more significant than the signified.

quatrain: a stanza of four lines, usually with alternative rhymes.

reified: turned into a thing and thus abstracted from the real social context that gives it meaning; for the cultural critic Lukács, reification is the basic experience of bourgeois life.

self-identity: the awareness of identifying oneself as a stable and singular subject.

sonnet: a poem of fourteen lines, classically divided into an eight-line octave and a six-line sestet.

stanza: the verse of a poem with a particular metre and (in rhymed poetry) rhyming scheme.

subjectivity: the state of being a subject in the sense of possessing selfhood, a self-identity, and recognising oneself as self-aware.

sub-text: not readable on the surface but capable of being deciphered, a meaning that is intended but not made overt.

syntax: the way in which a sentence is organised around clauses and phrases.

trochee: a metrical unit that reverses the pattern of the iamb by having a stress on the first syllable followed by an unstressed syllable, e.g. 'Hiroshima, Nagasaki' in 'The Morning After'.

trope: the figurative, not literal, use of language.

vernacular: when referring to language, the natural and everyday speech or dialect of a social group.

Further Reading

Tony Harrison, *Collected Poems* (Viking, 2007). There are various editions of Harrison's poetry but this is the most complete and up-to-date.

Neil Astley, ed., *Bloodaxe Critical Anthologies. 1. Tony Harrison* (Bloodaxe, 1991). A collection of material on Harrison's work, including his verse translations for the theatre, with some useful essays on the *School of Eloquence* poems and 'v.' The two Harrison interviews, with Richard Hoggart and John Haffenden are especially worth reading.

Neil Astley, ed., *Staying Alive: Real Poems for Unreal Times* (Bloodaxe, 2002). A superb anthology of poetry with an introduction that is worth reading as a way of approaching and enjoying Harrison's poetry.

Sandie Byrne, *H, v. & O: The Poetry of Tony Harrison* (Manchester University Press, 1998). As well as the poems, this study also covers Harrison's verse translations for the stage and his television work.

Terry Eagleton, *How to Read a Poem* (Blackwell Publishing, 2007). Although none of Harrison's poems is covered, this is an excellent guide to appreciating poetry and there is a lot that can be put to good use when it comes to reading and enjoying Harrison.

Luke Spencer, *The Poetry of Tony Harrison* (Harvester Wheatsheaf, 1994). A useful and readable study of the poems written before 1994.

Index of Poems

A Celebratory Ode on the Abdication of King Charles III 22
A Cold Coming 20, 24
A Kumquat for John Keats 27, 32, 34
Baghdad Lullaby 22
Book Ends 12, 17
Call of Nature, The 38–39
Facing North 35
Fire-Eater 27
First Aid in English 28, 29
Florida Frost 35
Holy Tony's Prayer 23
Initial Illumination 18–21
Laureate's Block 24
Marked with D. 10, 27
Morning After, The 1 27
National Trust 10
Nuptial Torches, The 24–26
Old Soldiers 28
On Not Being Milton 5, 7, 14, 27
Remains 9
Rice-Paper Man 49
Rhubarbarians, The I. 8–9
Shrapnel 26
Skywriting 36-37, 41–42
Study 11
Sugaring the Pill 42
Them & [uz] I., II. 3–4, 8
Two Poems for My Son in his Sickness 42
v. 13–18, 31
White Queen, The 26
Wordlists II. 12, 16
Wordlists III. 8

GREENWICH EXCHANGE BOOKS

STUDENT GUIDE LITERARY SERIES

The Greenwich Exchange Student Guide Literary Series is a collection of essays on major or contemporary serious writers in English and selected European languages. The series is for the student, the teacher and 'common readers' and is an ideal resource for libraries. The *Times Educational Supplement* praised these books, saying, "The style of [this series] has a pressure of meaning behind it. Readers should learn from that ... If art is about selection, perception and taste, then this is it."

(ISBN prefix 978-1-871551 applies unless marked*****, when the prefix 978-1-906075 applies.)

The series includes:
Antonin Artaud by Lee Jamieson (98-3)
W.H. Auden by Stephen Wade (36-5)
Honoré de Balzac by Wendy Mercer (48-8)
William Blake by Peter Davies (27-3)
The Brontës by Peter Davies (24-2)
Robert Browning by John Lucas (59-4)
Lord Byron by Andrew Keanie (83-9)
Samuel Taylor Coleridge by Andrew Keanie (64-8)
Joseph Conrad by Martin Seymour-Smith (18-1)
William Cowper by Michael Thorn (25-9)
Charles Dickens by Robert Giddings (26-9)
Emily Dickinson by Marnie Pomeroy (68-6)
John Donne by Sean Haldane (23-5)
Ford Madox Ford by Anthony Fowles (63-1)
The Stagecraft of Brian Friel by David Grant (74-7)
Robert Frost by Warren Hope (70-9)
Patrick Hamilton by John Harding (99-0)
Thomas Hardy by Sean Haldane (33-4)
Seamus Heaney by Warren Hope (37-2)
Joseph Heller by Anthony Fowles (84-6)
Gerard Manley Hopkins by Sean Sheehan (77-3)
James Joyce by Michael Murphy (73-0)
Philip Larkin by Warren Hope (35-8)
Laughter in the Dark – The Plays of Joe Orton by Arthur Burke (56-3)
George Orwell by Warren Hope (42-6)
Sylvia Plath by Marnie Pomeroy (88-4)

Poets of the First World War by John Greening (79-2)
Philip Roth by Paul McDonald (72-3)
Shakespeare's *A Midsummer Night's Dream* by Matt Simpson (90-7)
Shakespeare's *Hamlet* by Peter Davies (12-5)*
Shakespeare's *King Lear* by Peter Davies (95-2)
Shakespeare's *Macbeth* by Matt Simpson (69-3)
Shakespeare's *The Merchant of Venice* by Alan Ablewhite (96-9)
Shakespeare's *Much Ado About Nothing* by Matt Simpson (01-9)*
Shakespeare's Non-Dramatic Poetry by Martin Seymour-Smith (22-6)
Shakespeare's *Othello* by Matt Simpson (71-6)
Shakespeare's Second Tetralogy: *Richard II–Henry V* by John Lucas (97-6)
Shakespeare's Sonnets by Martin Seymour-Smith (38-9)
Shakespeare's *The Tempest* by Matt Simpson (75-4)
Shakespeare's *Twelfth Night* by Matt Simpson (86-0)
Shakespeare's *The Winter's Tale* by John Lucas (80-3)
Tobias Smollett by Robert Giddings (21-1)
Alfred, Lord Tennyson by Michael Thorn (20-4)
Dylan Thomas by Peter Davies (78-5)
William Wordsworth by Andrew Keanie (57-0)
W.B. Yeats by John Greening (34-1)

FOCUS Series
Emily Brontë's ***Wuthering Heights*** by Matt Simpson (10-1)*
George Eliot's ***Middlemarch*** by John Axon (06-4)*
T.S. Eliot's ***The Waste Land*** by Matt Simpson (09-5)*
Michael Frayn's ***Spies*** by Angela Topping (08-8)*
Thomas Hardy: ***Poems of 1912–13*** by John Greening (04-0)*
The Poetry of Tony Harrison by Sean Sheehan (15-6)*
The Poetry of Ted Hughes by John Greening (05-7)*
James Joyce's ***A Portrait of the Artist as a Young Man*** by Matt Simpson (07-1)*
Harold Pinter by Lee Jamieson (16-3)*

Other subjects covered by Greenwich Exchange books
Biography
Education
Poetry
Philosophy